797,885 Books

are available to read at

Forgotten Books

www.ForgottenBooks.com

Forgotten Books' App
Available for mobile, tablet & eReader

ISBN 978-1-330-32369-4
PIBN 10027220

This book is a reproduction of an important historical work. Forgotten Books uses state-of-the-art technology to digitally reconstruct the work, preserving the original format whilst repairing imperfections present in the aged copy. In rare cases, an imperfection in the original, such as a blemish or missing page, may be replicated in our edition. We do, however, repair the vast majority of imperfections successfully; any imperfections that remain are intentionally left to preserve the state of such historical works.

Forgotten Books is a registered trademark of FB &c Ltd.
Copyright © 2015 FB &c Ltd.
FB &c Ltd, Dalton House, 60 Windsor Avenue, London, SW19 2RR.
Company number 08720141. Registered in England and Wales.

For support please visit www.forgottenbooks.com

1 MONTH OF FREE READING

at

www.ForgottenBooks.com

By purchasing this book you are eligible for one month membership to ForgottenBooks.com, giving you unlimited access to our entire collection of over 700,000 titles via our web site and mobile apps.

To claim your free month visit: www.forgottenbooks.com/free27220

* Offer is valid for 45 days from date of purchase. Terms and conditions apply.

Similar Books Are Available from
www.forgottenbooks.com

A-B-C of Golf
by John Duncan Dunn

On Safari
Big Game Hunting in British East Africa, With Studies in Bird-Life, by Abel Chapman

Ourdoor Sports and Games
by Claude Harris Miller

Practical Golf
by Walter J. Travis

The Sport of Rajahs
by Baden-Powell Of Gilwell

Sports in War
by Baden-Powell Of Gilwell

Hunting in British East Africa
by Percy C. Madeira

The Complete Hockey Player
by Eustace E. White

Wild Sports of Burma and Assam
by Colonel Pollok

Athletics and Football
by Montague Shearman

Golf for Women
by Genevieve Hecker

The Young Folk's Cyclopedia of Games and Sports
by John D. Champlin

Football, the Rugby Game
by Harry Vassall

The Book of Athletics
by Paul Withington

Cricket
by A. G. Steel

Hockey As a Game for Women
by Edith Thompson

Lacrosse
The National Game of Canada, by W. George Beers

The Boys Book of Sports
by Grantland Rice

Tennis
by John Moyer Heathcote

Riding and Hunting
by Matthew Horace Hayes

PING-PONG

(*Table Tennis*)

THE GAME AND HOW TO PLAY IT

BY

ARNOLD PARKER

*Winner of the Queen's Hall Open Ping-Pong Tournament,
and of the Second Prize Table Tennis
Championship of England*

ILLUSTRATED WITH MANY DIAGRAMS

R. F. FENNO & COMPANY, : : 9 AND 11 EAST
SIXTEENTH STREET, : : NEW YORK CITY
1902

B610943
x

mbr

Preface

IN compiling this hand-book my main object was to put before the public in the simplest and clearest manner, the way in which the chief strokes of this fascinating game can be performed. No literary merit is claimed, but it is hoped that this little work will introduce a great deal of new interest into a game which is sure to stay, for as an indoor game it has not a rival.

Everything has been explained with great detail for the benefit of those who live far from the great towns and have not the opportunity of personally gaining knowledge of the game.

My deepest thanks and gratitude are due to Mr. W. E. Houlbrook for his valuable assistance throughout every stage of the work; to Mr. T. G. Figgis for his article on the state of the game in Dublin; and to Messrs. Jaques for permitting me to print the official rules of Ping-Pong. Without their help and that of many other friends too numerous to mention, it would have been impossible for me to have compiled this little manual.

ARNOLD PARKER.

Contents

CHAPTER		PAGE
I.	INTRODUCTION	13
II.	HISTORY	17
III.	IMPLEMENTS	22
IV.	GRIP OF RACKET AND FIRST STEPS	36
V.	SERVICE	42
VI.	STYLES OF PLAY AND STROKES TO BE USED	50
VII.	HALF-VOLLEY STROKES	56
VIII.	BALLS HIT NEAR TOP OF BOUNCE—	
	(1) FORE-HAND STROKES	64
	(2) BACK-HAND STROKES	77
	(3) MAKING THE BALL BREAK	84
IX.	GENERAL REMARKS ON PLAYING THE GAME	86
X.	IDEAS FOR HANDICAPPING	92
XI.	HOW TO RUN A TOURNAMENT	95
XII.	THE FOUR GAME	104
XIII.	PING-PONG IN DUBLIN. BY MR. T. G. FIGGIS	106
XIV.	PING-PONG FOR LADIES. BY MRS. HOULBROOK	110
XV.	OFFICIAL RULES OF THE PING-PONG ASSOCIATION	112

List of Illustrations

NO.		PAGE
	BACK-HAND DRIVE FROM RIGHT TO LEFT	*Frontispiece*
1.	METHOD OF LIGHTING TABLE	23
2.	CONVERTIBLE TABLE	25
3.	TABLE MADE BY LOCAL CARPENTER	26
4, 5, 6, 6A.	BALL PICKERS-UP	33
7.	BALL HOLDER	34
7A.	POSTS	35
8.	GRIP OF RACKET. FORE-HAND	37
9.	GRIP OF RACKET. BACK-HAND	37
10.	PENHOLDER GRIP	38
11.	THE SERVICE (1)	43
12.	FAST SERVICE (2)	44
13.	SCREW SERVICE (3)	45
14.	SCREW SERVICE (4)	46
15.	SCREW SERVICE (5)	46
16.	BACK-HAND SERVICE FROM RIGHT-HAND SIDE (6)	47
17.	BACK-HAND SERVICE	48
18.		54
19.	HALF-VOLLEY BACK-HAND	56
20.	HALF-VOLLEY BACK-HAND	57

ILLUSTRATIONS

21.	HALF-VOLLEY BACK-HAND FROM RIGHT-HAND SIDE	58
22.	FORE-HAND HALF-VOLLEY . . .	59
23.	FORE-HAND HALF-VOLLEY STRAIGHT DOWN TABLE	59
24.	FORE-HAND HALF-VOLLEY . .	60
25.	FAST HALF-VOLLEY	61
26.	THE ROUND ARM FORE-HAND DRIVE	65
27.	UNDERHAND FORE-HAND DRIVE	67
28.	FORE-HAND LOB FROM SIDE OF TABLE	68
29.	DIAGRAM OF SCREWBACK . . .	69
30.	CROUCH STROKE FORE-HAND . .	70
31.	UNDERHAND DRIVE FROM BEHIND END OF TABLE	72
32.	FORE-HAND STROKE FROM BACK-HAND SIDE	73
33.	FORE-HAND DRIVE FROM LEFT TO RIGHT	74
34.	THE SMASH	75
35.	BACK-HAND LOB FROM SIDE OF TABLE	77
36.	TAKING BALL WITH BACK TO TABLE	78
37.	BACK-HAND CROUCH STROKE	80
38.	BACK-HAND DRIVE FROM RIGHT-HAND SIDE	81
39.	BACK-HAND DRIVE FROM RIGHT TO LEFT .	82
40.	. . . .	83

PING-PONG

CHAPTER I

INTRODUCTION

THERE is ample justification for the publication of a volume on Ping-Pong, for, as far as I know, no treatise of any kind has yet been published about this fascinating and popular game.

Ping-Pong is a game which has been jeered at and called ridiculous, and articles have recently appeared in the Press which even go so far as to say that the popularity this game has attained, and the fascination it exercises over strong men as well as over women, is a sign of decadence in the people of this country. These articles must, I think, have been written by those who had never seen the game played well and had never tried to play it themselves; for, like another well-known game played with small white balls, it looks so easy till one tries to play!

Many people must have asked themselves, why Ping-Pong in so short a time has become so amazingly popular. The answer, I think, is easy, and will be found in the following facts:—

Firstly, all who have played must allow that it is an excellent game, excellent because it affords amusement for hours together, and because there is no small amount of skill required to play it at all well; this will account for much of its popularity. But there are other and, I think, weightier reasons. It has been called the "poor man's billiards," not that it resembles that king of indoor games any further than that balls are used in the playing of both, but because it supplies its place in the houses of those whose rooms and means are too small to permit the adoption of billards, since a very small outlay will purchase all accessories necessary for Ping-Pong; and if the proportions mentioned in a later chapter of this work be observed as regards height of net, not only can an excellent game be had on a small table, but any one can learn to play it well and will find himself able to do so on a larger table; play on a small table being excellent practice for play on the club-size table.

Further a great deal of exercise is obtainable from the pursuit of this game; and many a wet afternoon, be it summer or winter, which would otherwise be passed most probably in laziness with a novel, can now be spent enjoyably and healthily by playing a few games of Ping-Pong.

And last but not least, in answer to my question regarding the game's popularity, there can be no doubt that in the fact of ladies being able to play almost as well as men, is one of the chief reasons of its popularity.

In discussing the various strokes of the game, and the course the ball tends to take as the result of those strokes, I have endeavored to make the description of them as clear as possible, and to avoid mathematical terms. Moreover, it will be found that all the strokes described have been carefully illustrated, so that the reader, should he be willing, will be the better able to give them a trial. I have devoted a chapter to beginners, which I deemed especially necessary, as although the game is of some years' standing its light has, during most of these years, been hid under a bushel, and it is only during the last few months that it has sprung into popularity, and I venture to say into such popularity as no other indoor game has ever attained in so short a time. Therefore there are but few players who have played more than one year, and the vast majority have only played a few months, and must therefore rank as beginners.

Indeed, the game itself is still in its infancy, and there are many points which I mention in the ensuing chapters which must of necessity be debatable. I have given my own views on the matter, but experience alone will show if they are sound.

It must of course not be imagined by any intending Pongist who should happen to read this treatise that the game can be learned solely from reading a manual. Each stroke will require constant practice before any degree of efficiency can be obtained, and each intending player will have to adapt the strokes to his own peculiarities; for what is the best for one player is not necessarily the best for another. The qualities that a player must possess to excel are good nerve, sound judgment, resolution, and temper under control, together with fair sight and sympathy between hand and eye. Of these, some are the gifts of nature and cannot be acquired; others careful training will improve. From which it will be seen that, as in all other games of skill, there are bound to be some who will far surpass others in their play, and the less gifted must be content with mediocrity.

A chapter on the arrangement and management of tournaments will be found, together with a few hints to umpires. Also a chapter on Ping-Pong for ladies has been included.

CHAPTER II

HISTORY

It is not possible to write much concerning the history of a game that has had so short a life as "Ping-Pong." The earliest date I have heard mentioned in connection with the game is 1881. There is a rumor that some one started to play the game in that year with cigar box lids for bats, champagne corks for balls, and a row of books for a net. Most players, however, seem to agree that the game was first started by Mr. James Gibb about eleven years ago, and was published at his suggestion by Messrs. J. Jaques and Son under the title "Gossima," changed in 1900 into the name which has met with universal approval, namely, Ping-Pong.

Previous to the introduction of the celluloid balls, which was the feature of the game Gossima, the game had been in existence for some years as Table Tennis, which was originally played with a small india-rubber ball like a Lawn Tennis ball; but the game found but little popularity, nor did it under its new title until about two years ago, when the present seamless xylonite balls were invented and placed on the market.

The game sprang into popularity directly it was discovered that great skill was necessary to play well, and that the result of a match did not depend on the vagaries of a very badly made ball. This was about Christmas, 1900. For the next few months every one, more or less, played Ping-Pong, but summer coming on induced most people to put the game away until the present winter.

The boom started about September; clubs were formed everywhere, both in London and the provinces, and then a tournament was held last December at the Royal Aquarium, Westminster, for the Table Tennis Championship of London. The entry was enormous, numbering between two hundred and three hundred. Partly as a result of the success of this tournament the Table Tennis Association was formed, and about the same time the Ping-Pong Association sprang into existence.

It is not my intention to go into the merits of the two rival associations. All I will say is that it is a matter of great regret to all that there should be two governing bodies. The rules are almost identical, and it is to be sincerely hoped that a way will be found to bring the two Associations into one body.

The height of the Ping-Pong boom was reached during the tournament held at the Queen's Hall. Every paper had long reports and some of them leading articles. The majority of the articles and reports were, I am sure, written by people who had never seen the game played. I will mention a few that seem most interesting.

One paper said: "The Ping-Pong game is smaller in every respect than the Table Tennis variety, and strikes the onlooker as less scientific. One misses the *marked courts,* and the scoring is confusing."

Considering that Table Tennis and Ping-Pong tables are similar in every respect and that the method of scoring is identical, the absurdity of the above is obvious. Another paper mentioned a white waistcoat as making the ball invisible to the opponent. As a matter of fact it makes no difference whether black or white is worn, as any one who has played against an opponent in flannels will know. Then, again, the fact that a little boy (who, by the way, is sixteen years old) can compete with adults at the game is cited as a matter for scorn. There are many boys of that age who are much finer golf players than a very large number of men in the prime of life. In fact, in every sport youths will be found quite capable of holding their own against the average man.

I think it is a proof of the difficulty of the game that only one boy has come to the front. For, Ping-Pong being a new game, every one has played practically the same time, and a boy has had the same chance of practice as his elders, and, moreover, has all the adaptability of youth to help him.

There is no doubt that the game is being rapidly developed. It is generally agreed that the play at the last tournament held at the Aquarium was much better than that at the tournament held two months previously. The stonewallers, although prominent, were not so preeminent as on the first occasion.

Through the kindness of the proprietors of *Punch* I am able to conclude this chapter with the conjugation of the new verb " to ping." It appeared in their issue of December 25, 1901.

AN EXTRA-ACTIVE VERB.

On all fours with To Mote, Tu Be, Ta Boo, and To Week-end.

["Table Tennis" achieved its apotheosis in a Championship Tournament at the Royal Aquarium last week. It has therefore to be conjugated.]

PRESENT TENSE.

I PING.
Thou pongest.
He—ahem!—plays "table-tennis."
We are all champions.
Ye pay subscriptions.
They are outsiders!

IMPERFECT AND AMATEURISH.

I was pooh-poohing.
Thou wast using an eighteenpenny set.
He was wearing a club "blazer."
We were pitching into the umpire.
Ye were making your own rules.
They were having words.

PING-PONG

PAST (*last Season*).

I pang.
Thou pongedst.
He pung.
We groveled after balls.
Ye split your trouser-knees.
They burst their braces.

FUTURE.

I *will* ping, or perish in the effort.
Thou shalt "retrieve."
He will upset the furniture in his enthusiasm.
We shall annex the dining-room.
Ye shall go without dinner.
They (the servants) will bless us!

POTENTIAL MOOD.

I may turn professional.
Thou mayest take lessons from me (five guineas an hour).
She may show off her figure.
We may electrify Balham.
Ye may get "blues" (not "the blues").
They may win at the Aquarium.

OPTATIVE OR MATRIMONIAL MOOD.

I might become a "parti."
Thou mightest introduce me to thy daughter.
She might double her chance of marrying.
We might ping-pong into "Society."
Ye might "stand the racket."
They might hit it off.

IMPERATIVE.

Play!
Let him mop!
Let's have a drink!
Go it, ye cripples!
Game!

PARTICIPLES.

Present.: Ping. *Passive:* (not found).

Infinitive: To get into the Badminton Series and abandon the now undignified title of "Ping-Pong."   A. A. S.

CHAPTER III

IMPLEMENTS

The Room.—If possible, the room in which the game is played, should be as free from furniture as can be conveniently managed; tables and chairs in odd corners should be covered by cloths or rugs, otherwise the time and energy spent in searching for the balls will take a considerable amount of enjoyment from the game. The exercise in playing Ping-Pong being considerable, the room should be well ventilated. If possible, without causing too much draught, have both windows and doors open.

Lighting.—A good light is an absolute necessity if Ping-Pong is to be played with any comfort and skill. The light should be directly over the centre of the table, and as high up as possible. As it is most irritating to play under a flickering light, either electric light or incandescent gas burners should be used. Take care that any shade used does not cause a shadow on balls outside the table, otherwise players who drive from the back will lose sight of the ball after it passes the edge of the table. If the ordinary gas-jet is at the side of the room, and not over the centre of the table, the following is a very

PING-PONG

good method of fixing it up: On the wall at each side of the room place hooks so that a wire can be stretched between them, crossing directly over the middle of the table. An incandescent burner can be hung on this, and the gas connected with it whenever necessary by means of

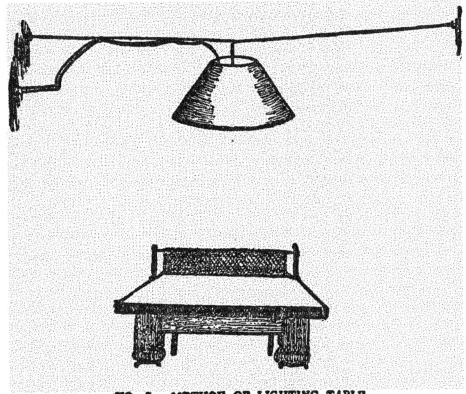

NO. I.—METHOD OF LIGHTING TABLE.

india-rubber tubes from the side burners. When Ping-Pong is not being played, and the room is wanted for other purposes, the wire can be taken down and all signs of the game removed. Thus an ordinary dining-room or drawing-room can be turned into a splendid room for Ping-Pong without destroying its use in any other direction. The light should be as high above the table as possible, so that it does not catch the eye of the players.

Tables.—For ordinary home play any kind of table can be used. Its size should not be less than 5 ft. 6 in. by about 3 ft., nor larger than 10 by 5, although many players assert that they get a finer game on a table 12 ft. long than on the regulation size, 9 by 5.[1] If the table has a large beveled edge, many more balls strike the edge than is the case with the ordinary championship table. These strokes should be treated as lets if the edge is very large. As the polish of ordinary tables causes the balls to bounce very high, the game resolves itself into hard smashing, and the finer touches of the game are lost. Therefore it is better to buy one of the table-tops, which can be had from several different makers at a cost of from $10 to $15. The best seems to be that made by Messrs. Slazenger. Any one not caring to go to the expense of one of these table-tops can get the local carpenter to make a top to place on the table in the same way as a bagatelle board. It can be made of ordinary boards glued together and planed smooth. It should have a joint in the middle, and be stained dark green or black. The cost for a top to go on a table 9 ft. by 5 ft. will be about $5 to $6. The tops can

---

[1] Height of net should be $\frac{3}{4}$ in. for every foot in the length of the table.

PING-PONG

be made to shut up without the net and posts being removed; in fact, it is no more difficult to fit up the Ping-Pong table than to put a cloth on. A very serviceable table designed by Messrs. Jaques for general use when closed is that shown in illustration No. 2. When opened out it forms a club-pattern Ping-Pong table. The largest size made when opened out is 8 ft. by 5 ft. When closed, it makes a very good card-table. The cost is $35.

NO. 2.—CONVERTIBLE TABLE.

Tournament Tables —For tournaments, of course, it is necessary to have tables of the regulation size; that is to say, 9 ft. by 5 ft., and the height of the top of the table from the ground must be 2 ft. 6 in. There are four makes of tables in use at different tournaments. (1) A very fine table which has a composition surface. These tables were used at the Queen's Hall Ping-Pong Tournament, held at Christmas, 1901, and, so far as the writer can judge, seem to be some of the best on the market. The ball comes away from these tables in such a manner that a good hard-hitting game is possible. The ball bounces nearly as high as on an ordinary dining-room table, but rises slow enough to allow the finer touches of the game to be brought into play. (2) A table which has a somewhat shiny surface. The ball on that account does not break very much and bounces rather high and quickly, making it something like the ordinary dining-room table so far as play is concerned. (3) The Table Tennis Supply Association table is some-

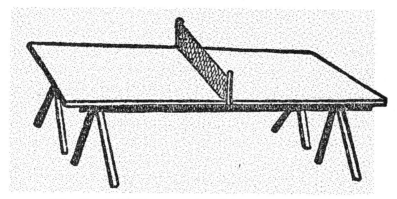

NO. 3.—TABLE MADE BY LOCAL CARPENTER

thing like number one; the surface, however, seems to be rougher, and the ball gets up very slowly, does not rise much, and is most difficult to hit hard. (4) Is the table made by one's local carpenter. This table will be made of boards glued together and planed smooth, and can have trestles made to support it as in illustration. The bounce of the ball varies according to the kind of wood used. The harder the wood, the higher the bounce. American white wood is, I think, the best that can be used in making tables of this kind. They should be stained a dark green, and have a white line painted round the edge.

Balls.—Originally the celluloid balls used for Ping-Pong were very light, and had a big rim where the two halves of the ball joined, causing it to bounce in all manner of unexpected directions. About two years ago a better ball was put on the market; it was heavier, and the joint of the two halves was almost impossible to perceive. Since that time they have improved very much; the finish is greater and the weight of the ball has considerably increased. This increase in weight was necessary owing to the size of the table, nine feet by five, as the light balls did not travel truly owing to the resistance of the air. In the chapter on the screwing of balls and their course in the air the observations have been made with the balls in use up to about three months ago; the heavier ball does not appear to be affected so much by screw or twist. Celluloid balls covered like tennis balls have been tried, but were found to be far too dead and heavy for a good game. Messrs. Slazenger will shortly put a greatly improved ball on the market. While of the same weight as the other balls it is much harder and can be hit faster.

The Racket.—Ping-Pong rackets appear to be made of every imaginable substance and of any size and shape. The Table Tennis Association, however, limit the size to six inches by seven, although the Ping-Pong Association do not. Some are almost square, others quite round others, again, pear shaped. The length of the handle varies in nearly every one ; in some it is nearly a foot long, in others it has practically disappeared, and some of them have a huge bulb instead of the ordinary handle. I propose to mention in detail the various kinds of racket used, with their chief advantages.

The Vellum Racket.—The vellum racket consists of vellum stretched over a wooden or metal frame. There are several kinds of racket on the market. In the old-fashioned vellum racket the wooden frame was very thick, and the vellum not particularly tightly stretched. With the improvement in the playing of Ping-Pong the vellum had to be tightly and evenly stretched, and the tendency has been for the rim of the racket to become much narrower. The quality of the vellum used in making Ping-Pong rackets has perceptibly increased, and sometimes it is almost as thin as paper, with a great amount of elasticity. Sometimes the vellum is covered with a thin coat of emery powder or powdered glass, the object being to obtain a greater spin. Some vellum rackets consist of a single strip of parchment strained inside a wooden frame. In one of them (an invention of Mr. Newman's) the tension of the racket can be altered by means of screws. The great objection to vellum rackets with a rim is that the ball in a large number of cases strikes the edge of the racket on leaving the vellum, its direction being completely altered. The best vellum racket is the Queen Racket made by Messrs. Slazenger, an improvement of which, to be called after the writer, will be on the market shortly.

The Parchment Racket.—The parchment racket is practically never seen nowadays; it is merely the old battledore; but as parchment alters so considerably under atmospheric influences, it has been found necessary to give it up. The imitation parchment, as it is called, is merely paper treated with sulphuric acid.[1]

Wooden Rackets.—There are many kinds of wooden rackets on the market; some of them are made of hard wood, such as ebony, oak or mahogany. Others again are made of pine or some other soft wood. The hard wood rackets are, as a rule, very thin. This is necessary on account of the great weight they would otherwise be. Some of the rackets have holes bored through them. This does not seem to make any difference to the way in which the ball leaves the racket. A wooden racket not, I believe, on the market, but which has been used by one or two players, consists of two thin strips of wood fixed on the frame used for the ordinary vellum racket.

[1] Real parchment is sheepskin dressed with chalk.

Covered Wood Rackets.—Some wooden rackets have parchment or vellum glued on the surface; others, again, have emery paper or sandpaper, or glass paper—all with the object of imparting a greater screw to the ball. There are also rackets on the market covered with cloth; and there is one make covered with an india-rubber pad, very similar to those one sees on many cash-desks to allow money to be picked up more easily than it can be off the smooth counter.

Metal Rackets.—The chief objection to the metal rackets is their great weight and the deadness with which the ball leaves the racket. There is only one on the market at present, so far as I know, and it is made of aluminium. So far as can be seen it has no advantage over a wooden racket, and many disadvantages.

The Glass Racket.—One racket on a stall at the Aquarium was made of glass surrounded by a wooden rim. Its weight was excessive. The writer has never seen any one playing with one, and cannot imagine it being of any use.

Cork.—Many players think a cork racket is the only thing to be played with. The ball comes away with a very great spin, and, in their opinion, all the objections to the wooden racket are overcome.

Gut.—A gut racket looks like a miniature tennis racket. It is very tightly-strung with very fine gut. All players I have seen using it seem to be quite novices. They are unable to control the ball in any way. This is, I feel sure, chiefly the fault of the racket, which does not seem suited to Ping-Pong.

Vellum Rackets compared to Wood and Similar Rackets.—Vellum, as everybody knows, alters under atmospheric influences. This is the chief objection to it. Several patents have been taken out lately to overcome this; the principle of them all is that of the drum or banjo, inventors trying to introduce the system of altering the tension of the vellum of the racket without increasing its weight, or having a rim, which ruins many strokes. The chief advantage of vellum, when in a proper condition for playing, is that a greater spin can be imparted to the ball. When the ball hits the racket, in the case of a vellum one it does not fly off immediately and time is given to impart the top spin necessary to keep a hard drive within bounds, and in fact time is also given for the direction of the ball to be altered after it has once touched the racket. In the case of wood and composition rackets this is not so; the ball leaves the racket the moment it is touched; no time is given for much top spin to be imparted, hard driving is very difficult, and the flight of the ball cannot be controlled with ease. The genius may arise who will be able to perform the same strokes with a wooden racket that are possible with a vellum, but at the present time players who use wooden rackets confine themselves as a general rule to half-volleying, and very rarely hit a ball after it has risen to the top of its bounce. As will be shown later on, this is a great disadvantage; the important point is not the time that elapses between the ball being struck by one player and returned by the other, but the time between the ball being struck and its striking the opponent's court. In the case of the player driving the ball hard this time is shortened considerably. Many of the finer strokes that are possible with a vellum racket are absolutely impossible where wood is used. Another objection to wood is that balls hitting the racket somewhere near the edge travel much faster than those hit at in the centre, owing to the greater spring. Players who use thick oak or mahogany rackets say this is not the case, but then the disadvantage of using a racket made of such a heavy wood is obvious. Metal rackets are hardly worth discussing, there are so few of them played with. The great majority of them are too heavy for use; one, an aluminium racket, has been put on the market lately, and seems to be the best of the metal rackets. The ball, however, seems to travel very slowly from such a racket, and bounces high from the table, giving a hard hitter every opportunity of bringing off his strokes.

To overcome the difficulty of vellum altering under atmospheric influences, the writer has lately taken out provisional protection for a racket that, it is hoped, will overcome all difficulties.

It will be possible to adjust the tension of the vellum, and the rim, which is the great objection to Mr. Newman's patent, will be conspicuous by its absence.

Ball Picker-ups, or Retrievers.—Many people having found the exercise of picking up balls too much for them, several instruments for picking them up without the necessity for stooping have been put on the market. I have given illus-

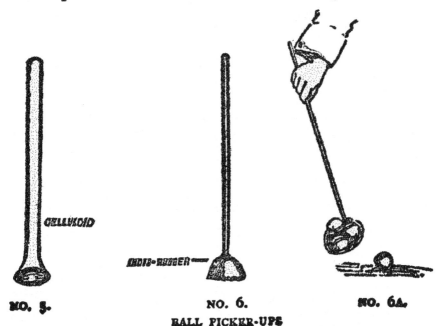

NO. 4.—BALL PICKER-UP.

NO. 5.   NO. 6.   NO. 6A.

BALL PICKER-UPS

trations of four of them. The first one consists of a metal frame at the end of a long stick. Across the front of the frame two pieces of elastic are fixed, and at the back there is a small net. By placing the rim at the end of the stick over the balls they can be picked up, the elastic preventing them falling out again. The principle of the others can be seen in the illustrations.

Ball Holders.—Those in use at the last Queen's Hall Tournament seem to be the only ones that

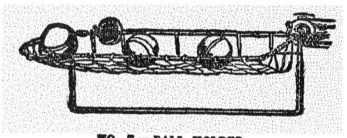

NO. 7.—BALL HOLDER.

are of any use. It is merely a wire basket fixed underneath the table so that it can be reached easily by the player, and does not in any way interfere with him during the course of play. It is fixed to the table by rubber suction disks.

Posts.—I will only mention two of the numerous makes of posts on the market. The first one is best suited for home use, the second for clubs.

(1) The posts are fixed in two heavy lead feet, which keeps them upright, and the net is fixed between. There is no danger of the table being

hurt by screws if these posts are used, but the net does not project beyond the sides of the table, as required by the rules for tournaments.

(2) The posts for club use screw on to the tables and project beyond the sides. They have extending bases so that they will fit any width of table. (See illustration.)

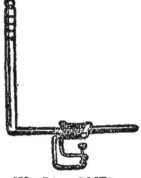

NO. 7A.—POSTS.

Nets. — There are three makes of nets on the market at present.

(1) White gauze net.

(2) Green gauze, with white band running along top.

(3) Net similar to a tennis net, made of string.

The green gauze net is the best for ordinary use, although the tennis net variety is very much liked by some who have tried them.

CHAPTER IV

GRIP OF RACKET AND FIRST STEPS

THROUGHOUT the whole of this book everything has been explained with great detail. Many players will think I have given unnecessarily minute instructions. My object in writing this book, however, is to teach, in the simplest possible manner, firstly, any one who has never played any game before the best way to play Ping-Pong; and, secondly, to give such information as will make any ordinary player equal to the best. Many points that a tennis player would take for granted any one else would be completely mystified about. How to grip the racket must be learned first.

Grip of Racket.—It is most important that the racket should be held in the best possible manner. Many players will say that the best possible manner is that which comes naturally to any one. This is not so in most cases. Of course there are born players, who succeed in spite of their peculiarities not because of them, and it is not wise for the average individual to copy them. First of all I will describe what may be called the perfect grip, and afterwards, one or two different ways of holding the racket noticed at the recent tournament will be discussed. Place the thumb on the vellum of the racket quite close to the head, the first finger being on the other side of the racket exactly opposite to the thumb. The three remaining fingers hold the handle lightly. The

NO. 8.—GRIP OF RACKET. FORE-HAND.

handle of the racket should be cut quite short; in fact, the little finger should just reach the end of the handle (see illustrations). If this grip be used all strokes described later on can be accomplished with ease; many of them may be made with the other grips to be mentioned below, but generally only a portion with any particular grip. Of course the position of the fingers varies slightly with each stroke.

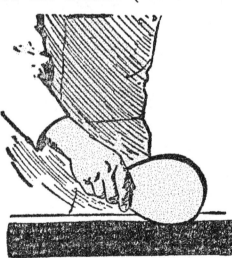

NO. 9.—GRIP OF RACKET. BACK-HAND.

This particular method of holding the racket is recommended as allowing these changes to be made without interfering with the accuracy of the returns. Some players, instead of putting the thumb and first finger on the face of the racket, place them straight down the side of the handle, so that the tips of both thumb and finger just touch the frame. If the wrist be exceedingly flexible this grip is almost, but not quite, as good as the one mentioned above. Many ladies use this particular method of holding the racket. Their wrists as a rule are more flexible than a man's. Some players hold the racket very much as you would a penholder; both thumb and first finger are the same side of the racket, the other fingers being below, the handle coming up between the thumb and first finger the same way as the penholder (see illustration). Others, again, instead of holding the racket quite close to the face, use a long handle. Players who hold the racket in this way as a rule play only back-hand or only fore-hand. They have small variety of strokes, but as a rule can drive a very hard ball when it comes in a suitable position. The great objection to a long-handled racket is the difficulty of taking balls aimed straight at the body.

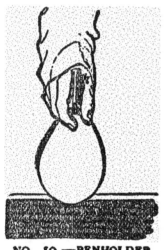

NO. 10.—PENHOLDER GRIP.

The above are the chief ways of holding the racket. There are hundreds of others which are merely variations of those mentioned. I must, however, again strongly recommend every one to use the grip described first, or at any rate some modification of it best suited to individual peculiarities.

Position at Table.—The best position to take up at the commencement of the game is one midway between the sides of the table, the distance behind it depending on the nature of the service. A player who only half-volleys naturally has to be quite close to the table, but one who both half-volleys and plays back can be continually shifting his position, making him a most worrying opponent.

First Steps.—Any one attempting to play Ping-Pong for the first time will feel most awkward. Tennis players, as a rule, think they ought to be able to play the game directly they commence. It is a great mistake. The game is so different in many ways from all others. The lightness of the ball makes its flight through the air very difficult to judge, and after it has bounced causes it to fall comparatively slowly, so that in most cases the ball is struck too soon, and is sent flying out of court. If beginners would only realize that there is plenty of time to hit the ball their play would improve rapidly. In starting to play adopt either the half-volley or back play, whichever comes most natural to you, but take balls both back and fore-hand. Balls on the left take back-handed, those on the right fore-handed. It is most important to commence in this way, as the single style game is most difficult to eradicate. Do not attempt to win strokes, but do the very best you can to hit the ball with the middle of the racket, and place it somewhere in the opposite court. The rest will come in time. Do not be disheartened if the ball at first rarely travels in the direction you expect it to go. It is impossible to learn the game all at once. There is no royal road to success. Before trying any of the strokes mentioned later on, try and keep up a rally of say 50 or 60 strokes. Be quite certain of returning the ball slowly before attempting to hit. So many players (particularly lawn tennis players) try to hit all at once. They do not keep the ball in, and consequently think it is impossible for them ever to do so when hitting hard. They then adopt a system of merely returning the ball, and assert that the stronger game is the purely defensive one. That is because they started at the wrong end; they should have commenced with pat-ball and trained themselves to hit instead of commencing to hit before knowing even the rudiments of the game. When you have got quite certain of returning the ball to the opposite court, then try and learn one of the strokes mentioned in the next chapter. When you have mastered one stroke learn another, but do not try and get more than one stroke at once. So many things have to be remembered in doing any particular stroke that failure will only attend any one who tries to learn too much at once. If possible, try to master the combined style recommended in the next chapter, and also learn, if possible, to half-volley and to play the back game. Some players will find it impossible to manage this. If their wrist is not flexible enough to play the combined style, I recommend the adoption of the back-hand play in preference to the fore-hand, as more variety of strokes is possible to a back-hand player than to one who plays fore-hand.

CHAPTER V

SERVICE

In spite of the great importance of the service, but few players have taken the trouble to study the question. Several services are mentioned below, and every player should try to acquire all those mentioned, and think out new ones himself.

Any one who is inclined to serve from above the waist should fix a stick lengthways about the height of the waist, and standing close to it practise serving underneath it.

There are a great many varieties of service in Ping-Pong. Very few players at the present time have developed a really hard service. Those that have a really hard service as a rule are very erratic, and lose more points than they gain in their efforts to serve an untakable ball.

(1) *To serve hard with accuracy,* stand about two yards behind the table, and, throwing the ball from a position a little below the level of the top of the table, swing the racket straight towards the point you wish to place the service. The moment the ball is touched the racket must be drawn across it from the bottom upwards. If this be done smartly, however hard the stroke

may be, the service will not travel outside the limits of the table. By turning the racket to the left or right the ball can be placed to either side of the court. This service must be practised continually; in fact, to get perfectly certain of, say, four balls in five, it is necessary to practise constantly for weeks.

(2) Another way of serving hard is to take the ball from the right-hand side of the body, using a similar action. This seems to be a more difficult stroke, but a harder ball can be served into the left-hand court than is possible when the ball is taken in front.

(3) Some players rely solely on the *screw service*. They make the ball break in either direction. There are many ways in which this is done. Some will throw the ball up, and, swinging the racket with its face parallel with the floor and from

NO. II.—THE SERVICE (1).

right to left, hit the ball underneath, causing it to break from left to right. By swinging from left to right the reverse break can be managed. This, however, is most difficult. The great objection to this service is the height of the bounce, enabling a hard hitter frequently to kill with the ball.

NO. 12.—FAST SERVICE (2).

(4) Others hold the racket (as shown in diagram No. 14) so that the face of the racket is at right angles to the table. By turning the racket round, using the handle as the axis, the ball can be made to break on either side. When the racket faces the left the ball will break to the left, and *vice-versa*.

(5) Another screw service is performed in the following manner· The ball is held in the hand a little way in front of the body, and the player looks at the portion of the court he wishes the ball to strike. The racket is swung with a circular, sweeping motion towards the ball, and hits it out of the player's hand without his throwing it up. The ball in this case travels rather fast,

and has a big break to the right. It is, however, very uncertain, as the position of the ball is guessed rather than seen.

(6) One player at the recent tournament held at the Aquarium served a very fast ball backhanded from the right-hand side of the body. He, however, did not use the grip recommended previously, and had no fore-hand strokes. His racket was held as shown in the illustration (No. 16). I do not recommend the average player to adopt this style of play, as the gentleman in question had a marvelously flexible wrist, which made strokes easy for him which the average player would find to be impossible.

NO. 13.—SCREW SERVICE (3).

(7) Many of the stone-wall players one sees in tournaments have no service that can be dignified with the name of such. They are content with getting the ball over the net somehow, and thereby starting the game. One or two of

these, or solely back-hand players, serve from the left-hand side of the body. One player, however, served an extremely hard ball back-hand. Leaning somewhat forward, and standing well away from the table, he swung his racket from under the right arm (he played left-handed) and hit the ball with tremendous speed. The service,

NO. 14.—SCREW SERVICE (4).   NO. 15.—SCREW SERVICE (5).

in the tournament at any rate, was erratic, but is perhaps capable of development. When serving, back-hand players have great difficulty in keeping the racket below the waist. (See illustration No. 17.)

General Hints on Service.—Every one ought to develop at least two kinds of service—a hard service and a screw service. After playing continuously against a hard server it will be found that, provided he does not change his service very considerably, the difficulty of taking it is no more than in the case of an ordinary pace service. If, however, in addition to continually changing the side he serves to, he also alters the pace and screws some balls, using the same action screwing as for the fast serve, he is almost certain to win the majority of his serves. Do not serve every ball from the same side of the table.

NO. 16.—BACK-HAND SERVICE FROM RIGHT-HAND SIDE (6).

Serve the first ball, for instance, from the right-hand part of the court across to the left, and then put one straight down the side. With practice this can be done without altering the position of the head. That is to say, while looking to the left the ball is served to the right. Until your opponent gets used to this he will be continually deceived, and frequently will never touch the ball. It is difficult, when standing on the left-hand side of the court, to serve a ball straight down the side line without bringing the racket above the waist. It is, however, possible to do so using the second service described above. Standing at the left-hand side of the court it will be found possible to place a screw service just over the net on the right-hand side. This should frequently be used when playing against an opponent who uses fore-hand strokes only. It is very difficult to serve a ball close to the net on the left-hand side. To serve a ball so that it drops about two feet from the net on the left-hand side is as good a stroke as can be expected. Occasionally, instead of serving to the

NO. 17.—BACK-HAND SERVICE (7).

sides of the court, it is advisable to send the ball straight at the opponent. This will take him by surprise, and the return, if the ball be taken at all, will be very weak.

Therefore vary the service as much as possible both as regards —

   (1) Pace.
   (2) Position at table.
   (3) Direction of service.
   (4) Screw or plain.

To take the Service.—To take a very hard service it is better to stand well behind the table so as to take it on the bounce and not at the half-volley. Services quite impossible to take at the half-volley become comparatively easy to an active player standing well back. Of course, the great objection to standing well away from the table is that a ball served short unexpectedly is difficult to take, but by watching your opponent carefully this can easily be anticipated.

CHAPTER VI

STYLES OF PLAY AND STROKES TO BE USED

THE styles of play adopted can be divided into three classes —

- (*a*) The back-hand style.
- (*b*) The fore-hand style.
- (*c*) The combination of the two.

Players who adopt either (*a*) or (*b*) as a rule play with the handle some two or three inches longer than that recommended in a previous chapter, otherwise without great agility a ball falling close to the net or on the side lines cannot be taken. One of the greatest objections to the back-hand style is the difficulty of hitting balls falling on the right-hand side of the court unless the grips (illustrations No. 10 and 16) be used. These grips, although allowing a player with a very flexible wrist to play a fast game, does not conduce to great variety of strokes, the finer touches of the game being conspicuous by their absence, and short cross rallies almost impossible.

With fore-hand strokes only a player has to move right across to the left beyond the side of the table to take balls falling on the left-hand side of the court, and to take returns falling close over the net on that side has almost to be a contortionist.

Fore-hand players stand naturally somewhat to the left of the court; indeed, some take up a position level with the side line, and with arm fully extended and a comparatively long-handled racket, take everything with a sweeping stroke. This kind of player, as a rule, develops a very hard drive straight down the table, but by putting top spin on the ball so as to keep it low all danger from this source can be avoided; and besides, a player good at placing can return every ball short down the side line on the player's back-hand.

It stands to reason that any one adopting a combination of the two has a great advantage. Players who can train themselves to play equally well back-hand and fore-hand have an immense advantage over those who can only play one way. This does not mean that any one using both back- and fore-hand strokes will always win against players adopting a single style, but that other things, such as natural aptitude, amount of practice, etc., being equal, the player who plays both back- and fore-hand will win.

To put the case more clearly, suppose that some one who only plays back-hand has a handicap of say 10. If he had learned to play both back- and fore-hand the handicap in all probability would be 5, or even less.

The principal reasons accounting for this are the following:—

(1) A player standing midway between the sides of the table can, provided he be of average height, with very little effort and without shifting the position of the feet, reach any ball wherever placed. If below the average, he, of course, will have to move slightly, but nothing compared to the running about when only back-hand or only fore-hand strokes are used.

(2) The firmer the position maintained the harder and more accurate may be the hitting; the necessity of constantly moving so as to be well placed to return a ball, when either of the single styles is used, interferes with the balance and causes inaccuracy. Moreover, since the player's relation to the table is constantly changing, so also are the table and surrounding objects constantly changing their position in his field of vision. This is both confusing and tiring to the eye owing to the constant effort necessary for it to accustom itself to the frequent changes.

(3) Since all the strokes possible to those who adopt the single styles are played in the combined style, it of course follows that variety of play and scope for improvement are much greater.

Strokes to be Used.

Now comes the question of strokes to be used. These can be divided into two main classes.

(a) The half-volley.
(b) All other strokes.

First must be discussed the merits of the two classes.

The great majority of players take every ball as often as possible at the half-volley.

In half-volleying a ball the stroke is not made at the ball, but at where the ball will be immediately after it has struck the table. That is to say, a player half-volleying a ball does not see it from the time immediately preceding its striking the table until the return has been made. While with the half-volley the ball can with great accuracy be returned over the net, it is almost impossible to hit it hard. Not only has the velocity of the ball, and the amount and kind of spin, to be accurately gauged, but being taken so much below the level of the net a the ball has to describe a much sharper curve than if struck when it has reached a'. (See illustration No. 18.)

A very hard service can be taken far more easily if the ball has had time to bounce, as its direction can be seen and time is given to swing the racket from one side of the table to the other, which, in the case of a fast placed serve is most difficult for a half-volley player to do in time. Also the angle at which the ball leaves the table shows the amount of spin to be allowed for in making the return.

By waiting until the ball has reached the top

of its bounce, or at any rate until it has been seen after hitting the table, a hard fast ball can be driven to any part of the court. The ball can be played "short" over the net and can be made to break in either direction. Players unused to the ball having any cut find a breaking ball most difficult to play.

Of course half-volley players argue that the ball is returned much quicker by half-volley

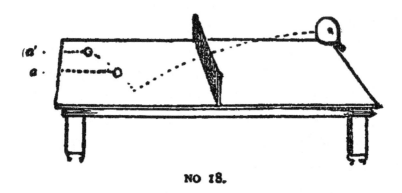

NO 18.

strokes. By this they mean that the time between the ball leaving their opponent's racket and touching their own is considerably shortened. But in most cases this is not the point to be considered. The important point is that the ball *after being struck* should reach the court opposite in the smallest possible time and in the least expected direction. Therefore it is not the time between the ball leaving one racket and hitting another that counts, but the time between the striking of the ball and its falling on the court opposite.

Of course an opponent who plays a single

style may at times be driven to move to such an awkward position that the stroke can be won by half-volleying the ball before he has time to recover. A ball when driven near the top of its bounce can be made to travel at a much greater speed than a ball half-volleyed, and is on that account all the more difficult to return, especially as the direction of the return may be varied at the last moment.

A defensive game is *chiefly* played with half-volley strokes, the characteristic of other strokes being attack. I say "chiefly," as it is possible by lobbing every ball to the back of the court, to "stonewall" for a time without resorting to the half-volley, and it is possible by quick half-volleys across the court to attack. A fast half-volley stroke will be described later on.

As both back- and fore-hand strokes should be played by every one, so should every player, who wishes to improve, cultivate both half-volley strokes and driving and lobbing the ball after its bounce has been seen.

CHAPTER VII

HALF-VOLLEY STROKES

To half-volley judge where the ball will fall, then swing the racket so that it will meet it immediately it springs from the table. To half-volley back-hand the position of the racket will be that shown in illustration No. 19.

NO. 19.—HALF-VOLLEY BACK-HAND.

(*a*) *The ball is some distance away at the left-hand side of the court.* The body will be considerably bent, and the forearm, wrist, and racket form a somewhat curved line, so that the position will be that shown in the diagram.

If the face of the racket is at right angles to the direction in which the ball comes, the ball will be returned in the same direction; if the angles made be not right angles, the direction taken will be on the side of the obtuse (or greater) angle, and the greater the obtuse angle the nearer the side line will the ball fall.

The distance the returned ball will travel before striking the table can be regulated by the angles which the face of the racket makes with the table. The smaller the angle on the side further removed from the player, the nearer the net will the ball fall, the greater the angle the nearer the back line.

The length of the return can also be regulated by the speed at which the ball is struck.

The nearer the ball falls to the body the more the position alters to that shown in the next illustration, but the grip on the racket is practically the same. The body, however, from stooping has become upright, and the arm is straight down with the racket at right angles to it on the left side.

NO. 20.—HALF-VOLLEY BACK-HAND.

(*b*) *Half-volley back-hand from right-hand side.*—When half-volleying with back-hand strokes balls hit to the right-hand side of the court the grip alters to that shown in illustration No. 21. The fingers have left their hold on the handle and stick straight out, and the racket is held by the thumb and first finger only. The ball can then be returned at the half-volley in any direction by moving the wrist backwards or forwards.

NO. 21.—HALF-VOLLEY BACK-HAND FROM RIGHT-HAND SIDE.

(c) *Screwback half-volley.*— A very effective half-volley, but very difficult to accomplish, can be made by bringing the racket sharply on to the table so as to hit the ball at right angles to its flight, making it travel quickly back with a spin that may bring it back over the net and which certainly will cause the *bounce* to be at right angles to the table.

The racket must be held so that the handle slopes away from the net.

The *fore-hand half-volleys* are performed in almost the same manner as the back-hand, but are more difficult to accomplish. Some players have asserted that it is impossible to half-volley fore-hand, but by holding the racket as recommended on page 37 and illustrated there, and keeping the hand almost on the table, the strokes can be performed with certainty. (See illustration No. 22.)

As the wrist does not move freely backwards, placing straight down the table a ball that comes from the right is difficult, but, with the body in the

NO. 22.—FORE-HAND, HALF-VOLLEY.

position shown in illustration 23, a fore-hand half-volley can be made straight down the table.

All these strokes can be made with the racket upright.

To accomplish them back-hand, the first finger and thumb hold the vellum of the racket, the fingers being straight out

NO. 23.—FORE-HAND HALF-VOLLEY STRAIGHT DOWN TABLE.

and not round the handle. The ball can easily be placed then by turning the racket, which can be accomplished by moving the fingers very

NO. 24.—FORE-HAND HALF-VOLLEY (UPRIGHT).

slightly, but the return is neither as hard nor as certain as when the first method is used. It is, however, a good stroke to use occasionally as the direction of the return can be altered by such a very slight movement that the flight of the ball is difficult to predetermine.

NO. 25.—FAST HALF-VOLLEY.

Exactly the same method can be used to make the strokes fore-hand. (See illustration No. 24).

Fast Half-Volley with Top Spin.

A very killing half-volley stroke is the following: Hold the face of the racket so that it inclines very much towards the net, and in striking the ball give a rapid upward motion. The ball travels fast with a very great top spin, but the stroke is very difficult to perform owing to the impossibility of foretelling the angle at which the ball will leave the table. (Illustration No. 25.)

As before explained, the half-volley seems to be chiefly defensive. Services and drives difficult to take from pace alone and not placing, can with practice be half-volleyed. Also it is possible to "stonewall" with great accuracy. But "stonewalling" is not the beginning and end of Ping-Pong.

Against some players it is imperative, particularly in conjunction with "lobbing," to be described later on. A half-volley player would often win rests otherwise lost had he at least one hard drive, as lobbing against a hard hitter is dangerous, to say the very least about it.

Every player will now see how necessary is the cultivation of as many hardkilling strokes as possible, and to kill a ball the stroke must, as a general rule, be made at the ball, and not at the place where it is calculated the ball will be at a certain time. The amount of screw and the elasticity of the ball (which varies slightly according to whether it falls on the joint or no) render the calculations very liable to error.

The player who is as good half-volleying as otherwise will be able to play each ball in that manner best suited to its velocity and direction.

In the next chapter will be found a description of strokes made either when the ball has reached the top of its bounce or immediately before or after.

CHAPTER VIII

BALLS HIT NEAR TOP OF BOUNCE

Fore-hand Strokes.

It is most difficult to describe accurately the way any particular stroke is made, but it is hoped that the diagrams and illustrations given will enable the reader to understand clearly what is meant.

Every one of course introduces little peculiarities of their own, but if the directions given be carefully followed, it is hoped that the strokes will be found easy of accomplishment.

Slight differences in the grip may make some of the strokes seem impossible, but with practice these difficulties can be overcome.

The strokes described are all possible, provided the racket be held quite close to the vellum. Every one is, however, recommended to adopt some modification of the grip shown in diagrams Nos. 8 and 9.

Many players use a few of these strokes, but very few use the whole of them. The fore-hand strokes will be dealt with first.

(1) *The Round-arm Fore-hand Drive.*—In driving from right to left, arm, wrist, and racket

are almost in a straight line, the face of the racket leaning slightly towards the table, and the ball being taken well away from and somewhat in front of the body (see illustration). Swing the racket towards the ball with the arm in this position, taking care that the racket travels almost parallel with the table. To do

NO. 26.—THE ROUND-ARM FORE-HAND DRIVE.

this the body must be considerably bent. The moment the ball comes into contact with the vellum, swing upwards so as to lift the ball over the net. The spin imparted to the ball by this movement will cause it to fall rapidly and keep low, and travel fast after striking the table.

The wrist can be used in combination with the

arm and body to bring the racket upwards. This increases the spin on the ball, but also increases the difficulty of performing the stroke.

If the ball bounce high this stroke can be performed without any spin being necessary. The racket, instead of swinging parallel to the table, moves slightly towards it. Great care must be taken that the ball is struck truly without any down cut, as otherwise the ball will fly out of court, the down cut causing the ball to rise. Strokes will be shown later in which the down cut can be used.

To place the ball straight down the table with this stroke the ball can be taken when it is level with the body instead of in front of it.

If the ball be played straight down the table from in front of the player the racket must bend back as far as possible.

The question of making the ball screw in the air and break after striking the table will be discussed later on.

(2) *The Underhand Fore-hand Drive.*—The ball is driven from straight in front of the body or close to it on the right-hand side, the arm moving at right angles to the table.

The racket is held almost at right angles to the arm and below it, the face being somewhat to the right of the hand (see diagram). Directly the ball is struck, pull the racket sharply upwards, chiefly by bending the forearm and turning the wrist so as to bring the racket above it.

This imparts the top spin necessary to keep the ball low.

The direction of the ball is controlled by turning the racket round on the axis of the handle by the movement of the forearm, not by moving it backward or forward with the wrist as pivot, as is the case in the "round-arm drives." Mov-

NO. 27.—UNDERHAND FORE-HAND DRIVE.

ing the racket backwards or forwards in the underhand drive controls the length of the return.

Although it is possible to drive a ball with greater pace and force by the use of the round-arm stroke, the ease with which the underhand drive can be placed makes it almost more difficult for an opponent to return.

The effect of a side screw on the flight and break of a ball will be discussed later on. It will be shown that the ball can be made to break in any direction.

(3) *The Lob.*—By a "lob" is meant tossing the ball into the air. This is the only possible way of taking some strokes.

NO. 28.—FORE-HAND LOB FROM SIDE OF TABLE.

A ball driven or served half-way down the right-hand side of the court near the edge, and traveling away from the table, must be taken in this manner unless half-volleyed (see illustration), or a ball just touching the edge of the table can frequently be taken quite close to the floor and returned high over the net. Care must be taken to return the ball well to the end of the opponent's court, as otherwise the smash to be described later on will end the rally.

A short player is frequently compelled to turn his back to the table and play the ball over his shoulder.

(4) *The Screwback.*—This stroke has been called the "screwback" not because the ball actually always comes back over the net, but because instead of traveling forwards in direction b it rises from the table in the direction a. The

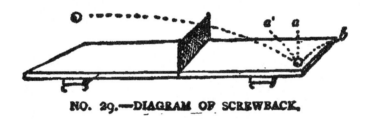

NO. 29.—DIAGRAM OF SCREWBACK.

tendency of the ball is to come back over the net, although sufficient spin can rarely be imparted to render this possible. It has, however, occurred.

This stroke is possible only when the ball bounces high, unless the half-volley described previously is used. Hold the racket somewhat loosely, the head being either above the wrist or at one side. Swing the racket parallel to the table rapidly towards the ball, and the moment contact takes place let the stroke take a downward swing, the racket being turned slightly back so as to hit the ball somewhat below the centre. This will impart a spin the reverse of

NO. 30.—CROUCH STROKE FORE-HAND.

that given in both the round-arm and underhand drives mentioned above.

(5) *The Crouch Stroke.*—This stroke is very difficult to perform effectively, but is one of the finest returns to a hard service or shooting ball.

A hard drive falls some few inches inside the

table and keeps very low. Bend down so that when the wrist is below the level of the table the ball can be struck overhand when it is level with or below the table (see illustration). The ball can be taken well behind the table in this manner.

It will help greatly if the right foot is drawn back, as in this position the body is quite steady. If the racket be made to describe a short circle from below the wrist to above it an extremely fast return is made, but great care must be taken to hit the ball truly without any cut. A very slight amount of cut from above downwards will cause the ball to fly out. Owing to the nature of the stroke a top spin is almost too difficult to attempt, although by lifting the arm during the stroke it may be imparted to the ball.

(6) *Playing Short Balls.*—This is a variety of the "lob," only instead of hitting the ball high into the air it is played so as to fall just over the net. It is most useful in taking balls that have hit the net and just dropped over. With practice the return can be made to fall on the table within an inch or two of net, and as the ball has been driven, in all probability from behind the end of the table, such a short return can only be taken very hurriedly.

(7) A very effective underhand drive can be brought off from right behind the end of the table after the ball has fallen below the level of the surface.

The ball must be hit as hard as possible, and directly it touches the racket the arm and wrist must draw the vellum sharply upwards so as to cause the ball to spin rapidly.

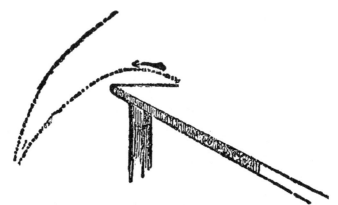

NO. 31.—UNDERHAND DRIVE FROM BEHIND END OF TABLE.

Its course will be very similar to that of the dotted line in diagram 31. It will be seen that the ball falls very rapidly towards the end of its journey, and shoots with great velocity.

The great objection to this stroke is that the ball sometimes goes under the table owing to the pull upwards not being sharp enough.

(8) *Taking balls falling on the back-hand side of the court with a fore-hand stroke.*—(This is a cross between a back-hand and fore-hand stroke.)

This is a very ugly and not very powerful stroke, and should be used only when it is impossible to take the ball in any other way. This

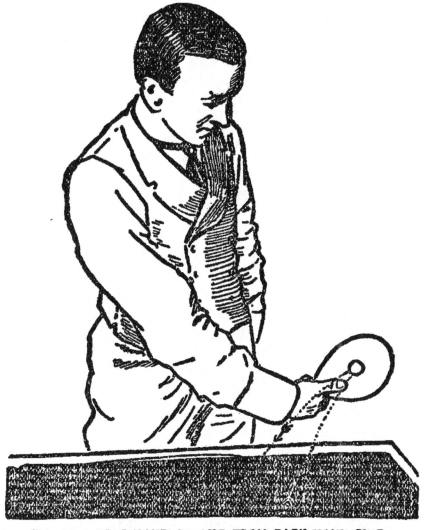

NO. 32.—FORE-HAND STROKE FROM BACK-HAND SIDE.

only occurs when the flight of the ball is misjudged, so that instead of falling on the forehand, as expected, it comes to the other side, and there is no time to turn the racket so as to make a back-hand stroke.

The position is that illustrated, diagram No. 32.

The forearm is across the body, palm of hand facing upwards, and the stroke is made chiefly by movement of the wrist.

The Smash.—When the ball bounces very high it can be hit straight on to the table, as shown in illustration No. 34.

The forehand drive from left to right.—When

NO. 33.—FORE-HAND DRIVE FROM LEFT TO RIGHT.

the ball bounces high on the left-hand side of the court step smartly across, moving left foot as far as possible parallel with the table, the right taking a slight step backwards; swing the racket parallel with the table so as to hit the ball with the racket facing the right-hand corner of the opponent's court. The ball will then travel with a twist that will take it off the right-hand side of the table almost at right angles (to the side of the table). It is possible to do this stroke when the ball does not bounce very high. In this case, however, the movement becomes a jump. Either the underhand or round-arm drive can be used Should it be necessary to play a straight ball without any break the underhand drive must be used unless the stroke is taken standing by the side of the table.

NO. 34.—THE SMASH.

Back-hand Strokes.

No. 1. *The round-arm back-hand drive.*—In driving from left to right back-hand, the forearm, wrist, and racket must be almost in a straight line, the face of the racket being at right angles to the table or slightly inclined towards it, and the ball must be struck when a considerable distance from the body. Swing the racket freely at the ball, moving the arm chiefly at the elbow. The moment the vellum touches the ball, give a sharp upward stroke, causing the top spin necessary to keep the ball within the court. It is very difficult to place this drive straight down the table. It can, however, be managed by turning the body considerably round so that, instead of being square with the table, it is at right angles to it. By drawing the racket from left to right across the ball it can be made to break from right to left. This is not advisable unless the drive is straight down the table as in playing across the table the break brings the ball nearer the opponent. In driving straight down the table this break can be increased by the action of the wrist. If the ball bounces high this stroke can be performed without any top spin. The racket, instead of swinging parallel with the table, takes a direction towards it; the ball, however, must be struck square so that no undercut is given, otherwise the ball will fly out of the court. Strokes will be shown later on in which the down cut back-hand can be used.

No. 2. *The underhand back-hand drive.*—The racket head must be well below the wrist, at right angles to the arm, and the ball can be taken from any part of the left-hand court. The face of the racket must incline towards the table, and the moment the ball is struck the racket must be drawn sharply upwards by the use of both wrist and arm. The direction of the ball can be controlled by turning the racket on the axis of the handle, and can be placed with ease to any part

PING-PONG

of the court. The length of the return can be regulated by the angle the face of the racket has to the table as well as by the strength of the stroke. Although it is possible to drive a much harder ball by the round-arm stroke, the ease with which the return can be placed by the

NO. 35.—BACK-HAND LOB FROM SIDE OF TABLE.

underhand drive makes it a far more valuable one owing to the difficulty the opponent has of prejudging the direction of the return. It will be shown later on that the ball can be made to break on either side.

No. 3. *The lob back-hand.*—The use of the

back-hand lob and the method of doing it is very similar to the fore-hand. A ball driven well out of reach on the back-hand side must be taken in this way (see illustration No. 37). A fast ball touching the edge of the end of the table can

NO. 36.—TAKING BALL WITH BACK TO TABLE.

frequently be taken by turning the back to the table and taking the ball from the position a yard in front of the body (again see illustration No. 36). Instead of getting square with the table by stopping and turning back, continue right round, taking the ball without stopping the swing of body. Much time will be saved if this way of taking the ball be adopted instead of the usual one of stopping and turning back again.

No. 4. *The screwback.*—This stroke can be used more frequently back-hand than its fore-hand counterpart, owing to the greater flexibility of the wrist in the necessary direction. Hold the racket fairly loosely and swing it straight at the ball. The moment before contact turn the face of the racket so that the ball is hit on the under side. This will cause the ball to travel slowly upwards, and on striking the table it will bounce straight up, or even occasionally come right back towards the net.

This stroke can also be done by swinging the racket at right angles to the table, so that the face of the racket is drawn across the ball from top to bottom.

No. 5. *The crouch stroke.*—This stroke is far more difficult to perform effectively back-hand than the fore-hand stroke; in fact, on but few occasions is it even possible. It only becomes so when a player has been driven a long way from the table and the return falls 4 or 5 inches within the court and shoots considerably. Step forward quickly with the right foot, and hit the ball as shown in diagram 37. Take care that the racket is not drawn downwards across the ball, otherwise the return will rise and go out of court. Owing to the nature of this stroke, top spin is extremely difficult, but perhaps possible, so that the ball usually falls on to the table by the action of gravitation alone.

No. 6. *Playing short balls.*—This is merely a

variety of the lob, in which, instead of playing the ball high into the air, it is struck so as to fall just over the net. It is practically the same

NO. 37.—BACK-HAND CROUCH STROKE.

as the fore-hand shot, the only difference being that it is possible to place the ball closer to the net on the left-hand side by the back-hand stroke than is possible in the other case.

No. 7. *Driving balls with the back-hand stroke from the right-hand side of the body.*—This stroke is a very effective and powerful one, very different from the fore-hand scoop-up from the left-hand side. The arm is turned round so that the

NO. 38.—BACK-HAND DRIVE FROM RIGHT-HAND SIDE.

back of the hand faces the net and the forearm and upper-arm are almost at right angles, and well extended from body, the racket being held at right angles to arm. It is possible to drive hard in any direction, but no side or down spin can be imparted to the ball. It is only necessary to use this stroke when forced by a very quick

NO. 39.—BACK-HAND DRIVE FROM RIGHT TO LEFT.

return to half-volley back-handed on the right-hand side of the body. If the return comes back

PING-PONG

quickly it can then be driven without changing to the fore-hand. (See illustration No. 38.)

No. 8. *The back-hand drive from the right-hand side of the table.—* Step to the side with the right foot and somewhat backwards with the left, when the ball falling on the right-hand side of the court bounces fairly high. Swinging the racket as instructed in the round-arm drive, the ball can be driven with great speed to the left-hand side of the table. If at the moment of striking the ball the racket be drawn quickly from left to right, the ball comes off the table with a tremendous spin, making it almost impossible for the return to be placed

NO. 40.

within the court. This stroke always causes the ball to break considerably without any wrist action. Owing to the wrist having more play in the direction needed, this stroke is far more effective than the fore-hand stroke from right to left. Occasionally, instead of placing the ball to the left, it can be driven half-way down the right-hand side of the table. The ball is then taken with the racket above the wrist. If done quickly this is a killing stroke. (Illustration No. 40.)

Making the Ball Break.

A great deal can be done in the way of making the ball shoot and break by imparting spin. I propose to state shortly the different ways of causing a ball to screw and the effect of the screw.

To cause top spin (*i. e.*, to make the ball spin in the direction of its flight) the racket must be drawn along the ball from the lower part upwards. This will cause it to shoot and travel fast as it leaves the table. When struck by the opponent's racket the tendency is for the ball to rise, and the return will very likely give you an opportunity for killing.

By drawing the racket from the top of the ball downwards, or by cutting across it underneath, the reverse spin to the above will be imparted and the ball will bounce perpendicularly, or even break back.

By drawing the racket across the ball from

right to left the ball will break to the right on hitting the table. The tendency of the ball when struck by the opponent's racket is to the left, that is to say, the opposite way to the break off the table.

By reversing this action the ball can be made to break to the left. Top spin, or the reverse, and a break can be imparted at the same time by drawing the racket diagonally across the ball.

The above directions hold good for both back- and fore-hand strokes. It will be found that a break difficult to perform back-handed is easy fore-handed, and *vice versa*.

CHAPTER IX

GENERAL REMARKS ON PLAYING THE GAME

In this chapter I propose to mention the chief points to be observed in playing a game of Ping-Pong.

1. Do not commence the game by serving too fast. Wait until you have got set, and gradually increase the pace of the service until your normal delivery is reached.

2. Vary the service as much as possible. Do not continually serve from the same place and in the same manner. The following are methods by which you can get variety of service. (*a*) By placing. Place the services so far as is possible at your opponent's weak point. If you observe that he is a fore-hand player chiefly, place them well down to his back-hand. Do not mind if the service is only a slow one, as the difficulty he will have in returning a ball from his weak side will in all probability give you the chance of killing with your next stroke. (*b*) Serve sometimes from the right-hand side of the table, at other times from the left and occasionally from the middle. In this way your opponent will never get used to the angle at which the ball leaves the table. (*c*) *Vary the pace* as much as

you possibly can without altering the action used in serving. One of the best ways in which to alter pace, and at the same time make the service more difficult, is by imparting the cut mentioned in the chapter on service. (*d*) A twist or back-cut service is also extremely useful, particularly after a very hard service, when your opponent has been led to stand well behind the table.

Develop, as I have said before, one or two services, and make certain of being able to place them. When serving take particular notice of the point to which most of the returns come. You will thus frequently be ready to deliver a killing stroke from anticipating your opponent's intentions.

3. At the moment of striking the ball, whenever possible, give an upward twist to the wrist. This adds pace, makes the ball go nearer the top of the net and come quicker from the table; also if the ball strikes the top of the net this twist will, in many cases, cause it to roll over.

4. Do not slog too hard at every ball; the primary object is to get the ball back over the net with sufficient pace and length to force a weak return. Do not start a game by hitting too hard, but start slowly and gradually work up to your full drive.

5. When your opponent gives you a ball which it is *possible* to kill, never hesitate from careful motives, but try to win the point.

6. In placing the ball always send it to the

spot most inconvenient to your opponent. The most inconvenient spot as a rule is that part of the court he least expects the ball to be returned to. Thus a ball straight at him down the table is very often a more telling stroke than one on one of the side lines. Also it is frequently more effective to place the ball to that part of the table his racket has just left rather than to the side it is being moved towards.

7. Do not lob against an opponent who can drive hard from the back line. He will in all probability kill every one of your returns.

8. Always anticipate, if you possibly can, where your opponent is going to return the ball. Do not move towards the spot you expect the return to come to until he has actually hit the ball, otherwise he may at the last moment change its direction, completely beating you.

9. Notice all your faults, and if possible get some onlooker who understands the game to point out any fault he may have noticed. Practice all your weak points as much as possible. Do not mind losing practice games, but leave off some of your pet strokes during practice, and try and take every ball in the particular manner that happens to be most difficult to you.

10. Do not when practising think that any manner of stroke or any kind of play will have no influence over your game. Always play your best and your hardest. However you have been handicapped try your best to win. Your constant

motto must be "Improvement." If you do not improve you will gradually become a weaker player. It is impossible to remain at a dead level: one must either improve or go back.

11. Do not be content with thinking of the game only when you are playing it. In spare moments try and think out some new strokes or methods of play, and then, when next practising, turn your theories to practical use.

12. Play as large a variety of opponents as you possibly can. You will then learn to attack many kinds of defense and to defend many kinds of attack. The experience gained will be of great use when playing in tournaments, and you are less likely to be upset by some entirely new method of playing or placing.

13. Deceive your opponents as much as possible as to the direction of your strokes. Practise looking one way and hitting the other. Practise moving your body so as to deceive your opponent as to the direction you intend placing the ball. With practice it will be found possible to move the body in almost any direction and any way, and at the same time to place the ball to any part of the court.

14. Do not play too much or too long at once. After playing for an hour or two the eye and wrist will get tired, and the play will become wanting in variety and sting.

15. Try practising by yourself. The following are three good methods for improving one's

control of the ball: (1) Stand about a yard or a yard and a half from an ordinary wall and hit the ball up against it, keeping it up as long as possible. The more expert you get in this the closer can you stand to the wall. This will make the wrist flexible, and is excellent practice in hitting the ball truly, because a slight screw put on the ball will make it impossible to keep up the rally. (2) A similar exercise to the above can be done by using the table instead of the wall. It will be found possible with practice to keep the ball bouncing on the table when holding the racket within three inches of top. (3) If the room is not too lofty practise hitting the ball upwards so as just to touch the ceiling. Keep this up as long as possible. This is a most difficult exercise, as the ball as a rule hits the ceiling too hard, making it impossible to send it up again.

16. Do not play when tired, either physically or mentally, as it is impossible to play one's proper game unless fresh, and to do otherwise tends to weaken one's game.

17. Make sure of easy strokes. Because it seems impossible to miss a certain return many players slash wildly at the ball, and frequently miss making a good return. Many games are lost through carelessness in hitting easy balls. The easier a ball is to take the more care must be used in making the stroke. If the stroke be lost not only does your opponent gain one point,

he also gains courage and nerve, especially if the game be a level one.

18. Variety is the great secret of success. Change your game so as to suit every opponent. Never play the same game against two different players, and if your opponent seems to be mastering you try another method of tackling him.

19. Always attack wherever possible. It is far less tiring to attack than to be continually on the defensive. Many tournaments have been won at Ping-Pong by purely defensive players. I do not think this will be so in the future. Lawn tennis in its earlier days was purely defensive; the great idea of every player was to keep the ball up. Winning strokes were unknown. In the present day something more than mere ability to defend is necessary to win lawn-tennis tournaments, and I feel certain that this will be the case with Ping-Pong in the near future.

CHAPTER X

IDEAS FOR HANDICAPPING

WHEN a stronger player is playing a weaker he should, if possible, in all cases be handicapped in some way, otherwise the strong player is liable to take no trouble or interest in the game, which is extremely bad both for himself and his opponent. There are many ways in which a handicap at Ping-Pong can be arranged:—

(1) The handicap usually adopted, or I might say always adopted, at tournaments, is to make the stronger player give points to the weaker—that is to say, the stronger player can use all his best strokes, but has to win more points than the weaker. The real object of a handicap should be not only to produce a level game so far as points are concerned, but also to produce good rallies, and make each player play the very best game that it is possible for him to do. This cannot be attained simply by giving one player a certain proportion of the game, but some system of handicapping such as the following should be adopted, to place them on a more even footing.

(2) Let the stronger player leave out a certain proportion of his most killing strokes. For instance, suppose his best strokes are those straight down the table, make him lose a point for every

ball he does not send diagonally. By making the stronger player do without his best strokes, he will be forced to improve his weaker points, thereby improving his game, while his opponent can play a better and stronger game, not having to fear so many killing returns.

(3) Make the stronger player place every ball to one-half of the court. For this purpose the court can be divided by a tape, or a cloth or something similar can be placed on the part of the table he is not allowed to play at. This again will improve his power of placing, and thereby strengthen his game. It should be arranged that if the player receiving points is weak on the back-hand, the stronger player should have to play to the back-hand side of his court and *vice versa*. The stronger player can also be made to play to the halves of the court alternately.

(4) Place an object such as a tobacco tin on the stronger player's court. The weaker player will be able to win many points by aiming at this tin. Even if he do not manage to hit it, it will be most disconcerting to the stronger player and cause him frequently to miss strokes owing to the proximity of this obstacle to the ball. The weaker player will considerably improve his power of placing by aiming at this tin. The position of the tin can be changed from time to time so as to induce him to place in every part of the court.

(5) Make the stronger player use the left hand in playing. This will not improve his game directly in any way, but it will help to develop the left wrist and the left side of the body. Many players find that with a little practice they can play almost as well with the left hand as with the right, and they will also find that many strokes are easier left-handed than right. In one way playing left-handed helps the right-handed player, as he has to move about very rapidly to take many of the balls, and in this way becomes able to take balls either back- or fore-handed, no matter where they fall.

CHAPTER XI

HOW TO RUN A TOURNAMENT

In this chapter I propose to put in the clearest and simplest manner the chief points to be considered in the arrangement and management of an open tournament.

Secretary.—The first thing to do is to get a good secretary. He must be a good man of business, able to make himself liked and respected, and should know all the points of the game.

Committee.—A strong committee is the next difficulty. It is as well to let the secretary approve all the people selected for the committee before they are elected. In choosing your committee the following points must be considered:—

(1) Capability of taking a portion of the secretary's duties from him and helping in the management on the tournament days.

(2) Ability to secure entries or sell tickets of admission.

(3) Whether any name on the committee would be a help or the reverse. It is decidedly unwise to have any one who is distinctly disliked in the neighborhood, even by only a small section of

the inhabitants, while the name of the popular person is worth a great deal.

Patrons, guarantees, and referee must also be selected with care.

It is most important that the referee should thoroughly understand his duties and can give his decisions with firmness.

The committee will first have to decide on the hall at which the meeting is to be held. Choose a place where there are good lighting arrangements. If play is to be by daylight there should be windows on each side of the hall, and if by artificial light the gas or electric light should be so placed that each table can be lighted from immediately above its centre. The hall should have plenty of accommodation for spectators and the cloak- and refreshment-rooms should be large enough for the purpose.

The date of the tournament has next to be fixed. The date should be about three weeks after the first circulars are out. The secretary, before the committee meeting, will have obtained the various dates on which the halls suitable are free, so that the committee can decide on the day or days without fear of the hall being engaged. The date on which the entries close must also be fixed. The date for commencing the tournament being decided the times of play have to be considered and the number of days the tournament will take. The latter will depend on the number of entries expected compared to the number of tables available. It is as well to have the ladies' events in the afternoon and the men's in the evening. This reduces the number of days necessary to get through the programme.

The different events to be held next requires consideration.

Handicapping in the present state of the game is almost impossible, so that all the events should be scratch ones.

Two events should always be held—one for ladies and another for gentlemen; and if there is time mixed doubles on the system explained in this book might be included.

Another point to be considered is whether the tournament should be held under Table Tennis or Ping-Pong rules, or if ordinary lawn-tennis score should be adopted and special rules made.

The next question to be considered is whether the tournament should be on the American system in sections or a knock-out tournament. This will depend on the number of days it is proposed to devote to the tournament. A knock-out tournament of three games of twenty points is a better test of a player's ability, but a larger entry will be received if the American system be adopted.

It will be found as a general rule that fifteen games of twenty points can be played on each table every hour.

The question of entry fee comes next; 60 cents, including admission, is, I think, sufficient for all local tournaments. The fee should be increased for tournaments held at places like the Queen's Hall or the Royal Aquarium. The value of the prizes will of course depend on the funds expected to be received. If possible the whole of the money received as entry fees should be spent in prizes.

The price of admission to view a tournament will of course depend to a certain extent on the neighborhood. I think that 25 cents for admission, with another 25 cents for a front seat round any table, is a fair and reasonable charge.

The above points should be embodied in a circular and sent to all Ping-Pong or Table Tennis clubs within a reasonable distance, as well as to any one the committee think likely to enter, obtain entries or sell tickets. Big bills should also be printed and shopkeepers induced to display them. They might also be persuaded to sell tickets if given free admittance.

The *Secretary* should, as far as possible, divide his duties among his committee, keeping, of course, supreme control.

For instance, committeeman No. 1 should have charge of the refreshments, and should be in the first round, and the winner plays responsible for all arrangements connected with them.

No. 2 should have the preparation of the hall for the tournament. He must see that sufficient tables are provided, that the lighting of each is good, that the nets and posts are properly fixed.

He should make arrangements for keeping a clear space round each table, so that players are not hampered by the spectators, and each table should be clearly numbered. Also he must take care that there is an abundant supply of balls of good quality. Seats should be placed round each table (about two or three rows are sufficient), so that people can watch the game comfortably.

No. 3 should have charge of the umpires and scoring. He must make arrangements for the results of each game being clearly posted up and must generally see that the umpires are efficient and that time is not wasted in playing off the matches.

No. 4 should have charge of competitors. He must see that they are wearing their numbers as printed on the programmes, that they know where to play, and he must take care that they are acquainted with any special rules the committee have made, such as length of game, etc. Also, if the tournament is a knock-out one, he must see that they play the proper people and that no table is left vacant.

The Draw.—Directly all the entries have been received, the draw should be made. All the names should be written on slips of paper, and when well mixed together drawn one by one. The names as they are drawn should be entered in lists.

First, we will suppose that the tournament is a knock-out one. All the byes should be in the first round. To find out how many byes there should be, take the difference between the power of two next above the number of entries and the number of entries. This will give the number of byes. Thus, suppose the number of entries is 17. The power of two next above 17 is 32, $32 - 17 = 15$. The number of byes is therefore 15. The programmes should be printed as shown in diagram. What is meant may be clearly seen on p. 101.

It will be seen that No. 9 plays No. 10 No. 11 in the second round. There are thus eight pairs in the second round. Had there been eighteen entries, No. 11 would have played No. 12 in the first round, and the winner have played winner of Nos. 9 and 10 in second round, No. 13 playing 14 in second round, and so on.

The byes are always at the top and bottom of the list, those whose names are drawn in the middle always having the extra round to play.

If the tournament is an American one in, say, three sections, then Nos. 1-6 would form one section, Nos. 7-12 another, and Nos. 13-17 another. The winners of each section then play off for first, second, and third prizes.

When the entries are very large the winners of the first round of sections are drawn into new sections, and the winners of these sections play for places.

At the Table Tennis Tournament, held at the Royal Aquarium during January, the winners of

PING-PONG

Name.　First Round.　Second Round.　Third Round.　Final.

1 ——
2 —— } bye

3 ——
4 —— } bye

5 ——
6 —— } bye

7 ——
8 —— } bye

9 ——
10 ——
11 —— bye

12 ——
13 —— } bye

14 ——
15 —— } bye

16 ——
17 —— } bye

the first twenty-four sections were drawn into four sections of six players. The winner of section A played the winner of D for right to play in final, and the winner of B played winner of C. The winners played for first and second prizes in final, and the losers for third and fourth prizes.

If the tournament is to last for more than two days, each competitor should be advised as soon as possible after the draw of the day he is to play. Arrangements should be made for admitting competitors into the hall early, so that they can get some practice before playing. It would be as well if some committeeman were appointed to see that only competitors playing the same evening were practising, otherwise they often experience some difficulty in getting a table to play on.

The Referee's duties are to decide all doubtful questions of law and any disputes that may arise during play. In the case of a knock-out tournament he will also have to keep all the results and arrange all the matches in the different rounds.

The duties of the Umpire are the following:

To see that the game is played strictly in accordance with the rules. Great care and judgment must be used over the following points:—

(1) The service. Every service not *underhand*, *not below the waist* or *not behind the end of the table* must be called a *fault* immediately.

(2) The score must be called distinctly after every point.

(3) In giving a "let" when the player is obstructed by spectators.

(4) If doubtful whether the ball touched table or not the umpire should call a let.

(5) The result must be handed into the referee, and care taken that the correct result is given.

(6) The umpire must not be influenced by anything the spectators say. Some umpires give their decisions according to the opinions of the onlookers rather than their own judgment.

(7) If the tournament is an American one in sections, the umpire will have to arrange the order of play in the section of which he is umpire. The players should play in regular rotation.

If the secretary can divide his duties among his committee on the day of the tournament as suggested above, all his energies can be devoted to supervising things in general, and looking after the spectators and the Press representatives.

CHAPTER XII

THE FOUR GAME

The following is a description of Ping-Pong for four players. So far as I know, Hendon is the only place where the game is played in this manner.

Divide the table down the centre by a piece of tape. The table will then be divided into four courts.

The four players each defend one half court, A and B being partners and C and D. Suppose A commences to serve. The service must fall into C's court, and must be taken by him and returned into B's court, who must return it to D, who sends it back to A, and so on.

If the ball falls into the wrong half-court, or is taken by the wrong player, the point is lost. This stops poaching. Any ball falling on the tape counts as right. After each has served once the rotation changes, A serving to D, who returns to B, and so on. Every one thus plays straight and diagonally.

This game greatly improves a player's power of placing.

A tape is better than a painted line, for not

only can it be removed for singles, but line balls can be more easily judged owing to the different sound the ball makes when it strikes the tape. A couple of drawing-pins fix the tape perfectly.

CHAPTER XIII

PING-PONG IN DUBLIN

Mr. T. G. Figgis, of the Mount Temple Ping-Pong Club, Dublin, has very kindly written the following article for me on the state of Ping-Pong in Dublin.

I may mention that Mr. Figgis is one of the strongest players in Dublin, and that, in addition to a tremendously fast service, he has a powerful round-arm fore-hand drive that it is almost impossible to take.

Mr. Figgis says:—

"For a game introduced into Dublin within the comparatively recent period of six months, nothing is more surprising than the rapidity with which Ping-Pong has sprung into popularity. To use an advertising phrase, it 'supplies a long-felt want' in the way of winter amusement. Apart from billards, it is by far the best indoor game hitherto invented, while the fact of its cheapness and adaptability brings it within the reach of everybody.

"Will the Ping-Pong craze continue? is a question we constantly hear. I would unhesitatingly reply that it has come to stay. At the commencement of its career numerous cynics were met with, who pooh-poohed the game as suitable only for girls and children, but recent developments have shown that such is far from being the case, and the limits of the scientific possibilities of the game have not yet apparently been attained. At an early stage in the history of the game in Dublin, clubs sprang up rapidly all over the city and suburbs. The Mount Temple Club, I should say, can lay claim to having the best exponents of the game, and Mr. A. K. Hodges, who is a member of this club, may fairly be considered the best all-round player in Dublin. He has won about four or five open tournaments, and, I think, been beaten only once in an open competition. His style of play is very neat, and he confines himself principally to front-hand half-volleying, though when opportunity arises he gets in some smashing strokes. A peculiarity of his stroke, wherein he differs from most players, is that he takes balls on both corners of the table with the front part of the racket. How he can twist the wrist of his right hand to take a left-hand corner ball in this manner is a marvel, and the stroke, to be appreciated, needs only to be tried.

"We have also some very hard hitters, who go in almost entirely for the slogging game, amongst whom I might mention Mr. H. Rooke, who is very little behind Mr. Hodges. This kind of game, from a spectator's point of view, is much more interesting, though perhaps not quite so certain or safe a game as the steady half-volley.

"A hard serve is an important factor in a game, and if delivered indiscriminately to both corners of the table, is often unplayable. The half-volley, in my opinion, is the only way to deal with such strokes.

"Perhaps one of the best managed tournaments up to the present was one held in the Sackville Hall, Sackville Street, on the 6th and 7th January, under the auspices of the Presbyterian Association. The tournament was conducted under the rules of the Ping-Pong Association, and the tables were of brown compo board, 9 ft. by 4 ft. by 30 in. There were about 120 entries, and some exciting and brilliant play was witnessed by a large audience. Hodges eventually worked off all his opponents, and got first prize in the Gents Open Singles, the second going to Mr. S. L. Fry, a well-known tennis player, and also a member of the Mount Temple Club.

"The largest tournament up to now will be held on the 31st Jan. and February 1st at the Earlsfort Rink, when prizes to the value of £25 will be offered. It will be worked on the same lines as the tournament held at the Queen's Hall, London, and as all the best players in the city will probably enter, one will be in a position to judge of the respective merits of their play.

"At present an effort is being made to organize a match between this city and Belfast, where I understand there are a number of first-class players, and where the enthusiasm for the game is no less than here.

"In the northern Athens I am told they use principally wooden rackets. Here, however, all good players advocate the vellum racket, which is held very close to the head. I have never yet seen a really first-class player of the game use a wooden racket, and many people who have tried them have resorted again to the vellum.

"What the future of Ping-Pong may be in Dublin I cannot say, but I am confident that it will still further gain in public favor, as the tendency indicates that the more it is played the better it is appreciated."

CHAPTER XIV

PING-PONG FOR LADIES

By Mrs. Houlbrook, winner Second Prize Queen's Hall Tournament.

THIS chapter, written specially for ladies, must of necessity be short, and the few remarks I shall make will consist in large part in a few hints as to the costume which will be found most suitable and best calculated to allow of freedom of movement and a thorough enjoyment of the game. For as regards strokes, service, etc., there is nothing further to be added, as all that has been written in other parts of this volume applies equally to men and women.

There is little to say about dress; in fact, one of the great advantages which the game possesses for women is that it can be played in almost any variety of costume with comfort, if the following few points be observed.

The *skirt* should be fairly short, that is to say it should be of the length of an ordinary walking skirt and clear the ground all round. Trains are to be avoided, as in the course of a keen game the most skilled manipulator of that form of skirt will most surely step on it—an accident which cannot fail to unsteady the balance somewhat, even if it does not actually cause a fall, and so an important stroke may be lost. Moreover, it will in all probability injure the skirt, the knowledge of which injury will not tend to help the player to maintain the equilibrium of her temper, which has already been sorely tried by the loss of an important stroke.

Bodice.—The sleeves should be long and sufficiently loose to permit freedom of movement.

Ornaments.—With regard to these, I have not found that there is any need to remove either rings or bracelets; but I strongly advise that long chains round the neck should be dispensed with, as the hand or racket is very apt to become entangled in it.

Boots and Shoes.—These are the only other articles of apparel I consider require mention. I—and many others have told me the same thing—consider that patent leather should be avoided, as boots or shoes made of this are very tiring to the feet.

And whatever kind of boot or shoe be worn, low heels will be found the most comfortable, as high French heels tire the ankles and feet.

In conclusion, let me exhort ladies who intend to take up this charming and fascinating pastime to give it the serious attention it merits. For there is no other game which offers so many possibilities to women to excel and play on equal terms with men.

CHAPTER XV

LAWS OF PING-PONG[1]

NOTE.—Reprinted by kind permission of Messrs. John Jaques and Son, Ltd., and Hamley Bros., the owners of the copyright, by whom all rights are reserved.

1.—The game is for two players. They shall stand one at each end of the table. The player who first delivers the ball shall be called the server, and the other the striker-out.

2.—The server shall stand behind the end and within the limits of the width of the table.

3.—The service shall be strictly underhand, and from behind the table; that is to say, at the time of striking the ball the racket may not be over the table, and no part of the racket, except the handle, may be above the *waist*.

4.—The ball served must drop on the table-top beyond the net, and is then in play. If it drops into the net or off the table it is called a "fault," and counts to the striker-out.

5.—There is no second service, *except* when the ball touches the net or posts in passing over *and drops on the table, beyond the net* when it is called "a let," and another service is allowed.

---

[1] The new laws will be published shortly. Although differently worded to those printed, they have the same meaning, except Rule 2, which will read that the *ball* and not the *server* shall be within the limits of the width of the table.

6.—If the ball in play strike any object above or round the table before it drops on the table (net or posts excepted), it counts against the striker.

7.—The server wins a stroke if the striker-out fails to return the service, or the ball in play.

8.—The striker-out wins a stroke if the server serve a "fault," or fails to return the ball in play so that it falls off the table.

9.—No volleying is allowed, whether intentional or otherwise, and if any ball shall be touched before striking the table it counts against the player touching it; should, however, a ball pass the limits of the table without dropping on it is dead, and counts against the striker.

Scoring.

The method of scoring shall be by points, 20 points up constituting a game, the service changing after each five points scored. Should the score reach 19 all, it shall be called "game all," and the best of 5 points shall decide the game.